Altitudes *of the* Alps

SWITZERLAND'S TICINO REGION

A TRAVEL PHOTO ART BOOK

LAINE CUNNINGHAM

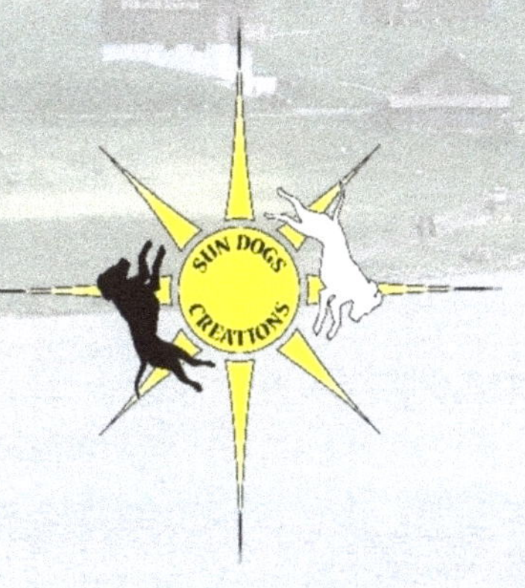

Altitudes of the Alps

Switzerland's Ticino Region

A Travel Photo Art Book

Published by Sun Dogs Creations
Changing the World One Book at a Time
Print ISBN: 9781946732897

Cover Design by Angel Leya

THE TRAVEL PHOTO ART SERIES

Bikes of Berlin

Necropolises of New Orleans I & II

Ruins of Rome I & II

Ancients of Assisi I & II

Panoramas of Portugal

Nuances of New York

Glimpses of Germany

Impressions of Italy

Altitudes of the Alps

Utopia of the Unicorn

Knights Through the Ages

STEEPLECHASE

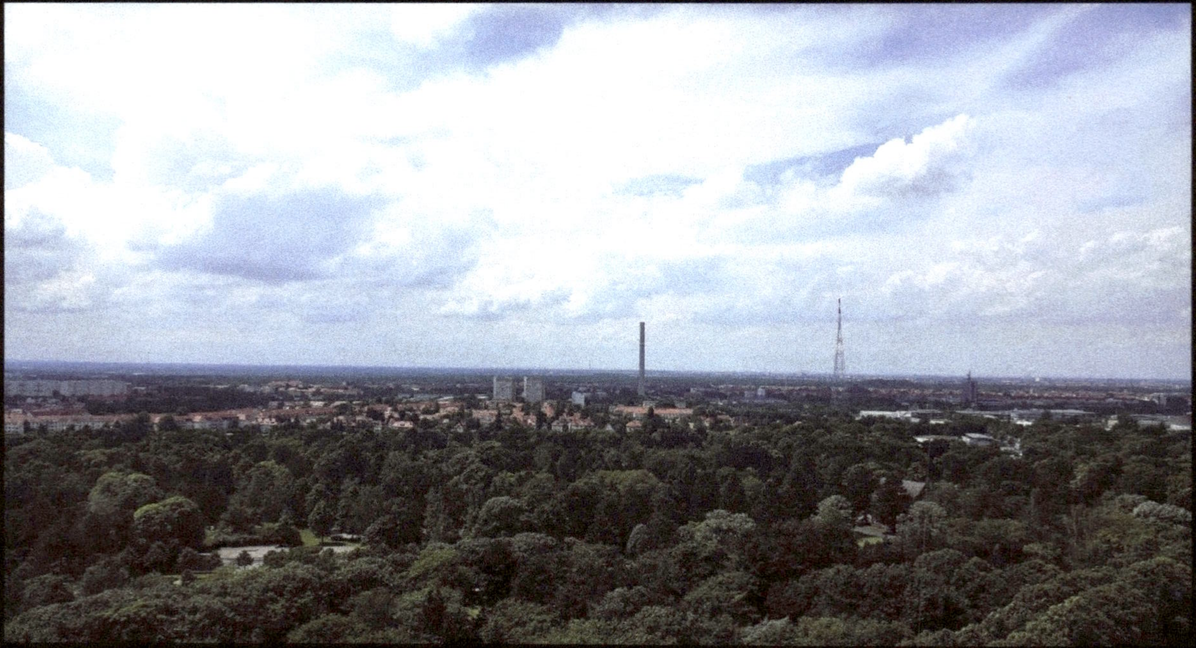

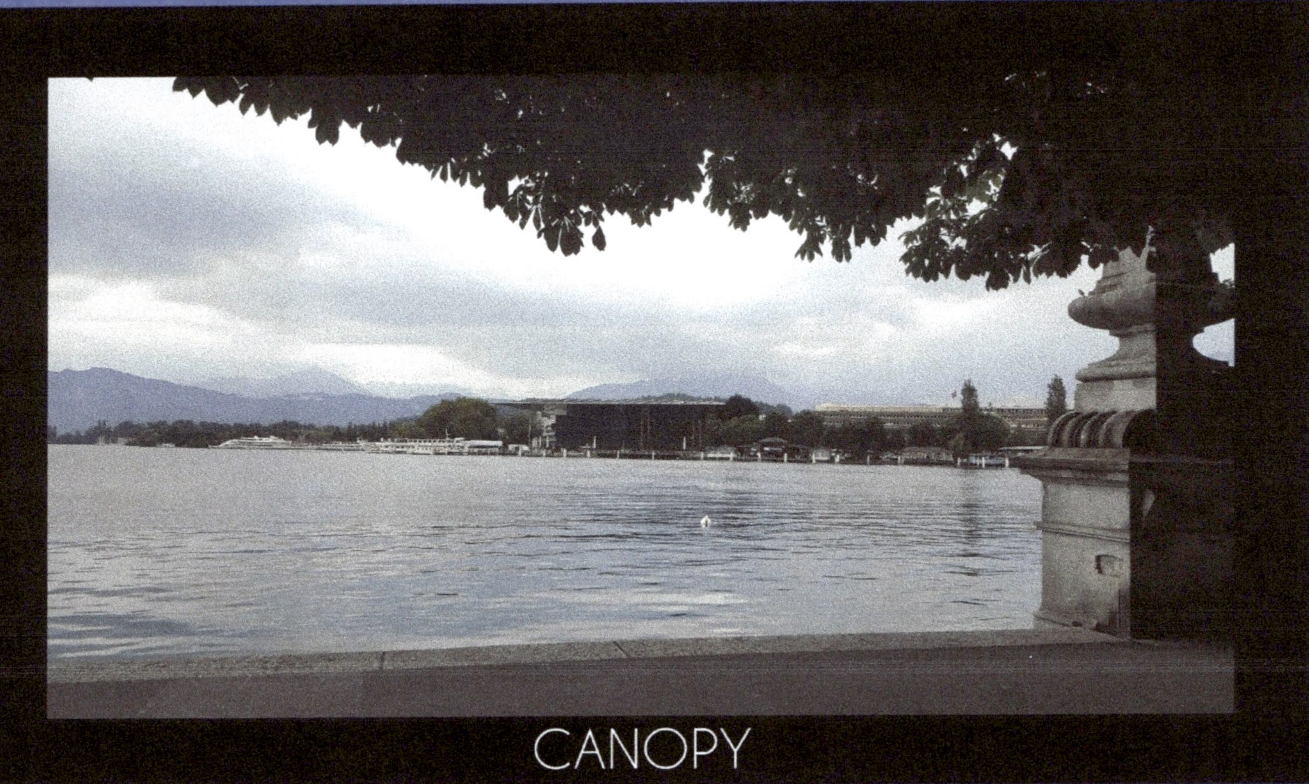
CANOPY

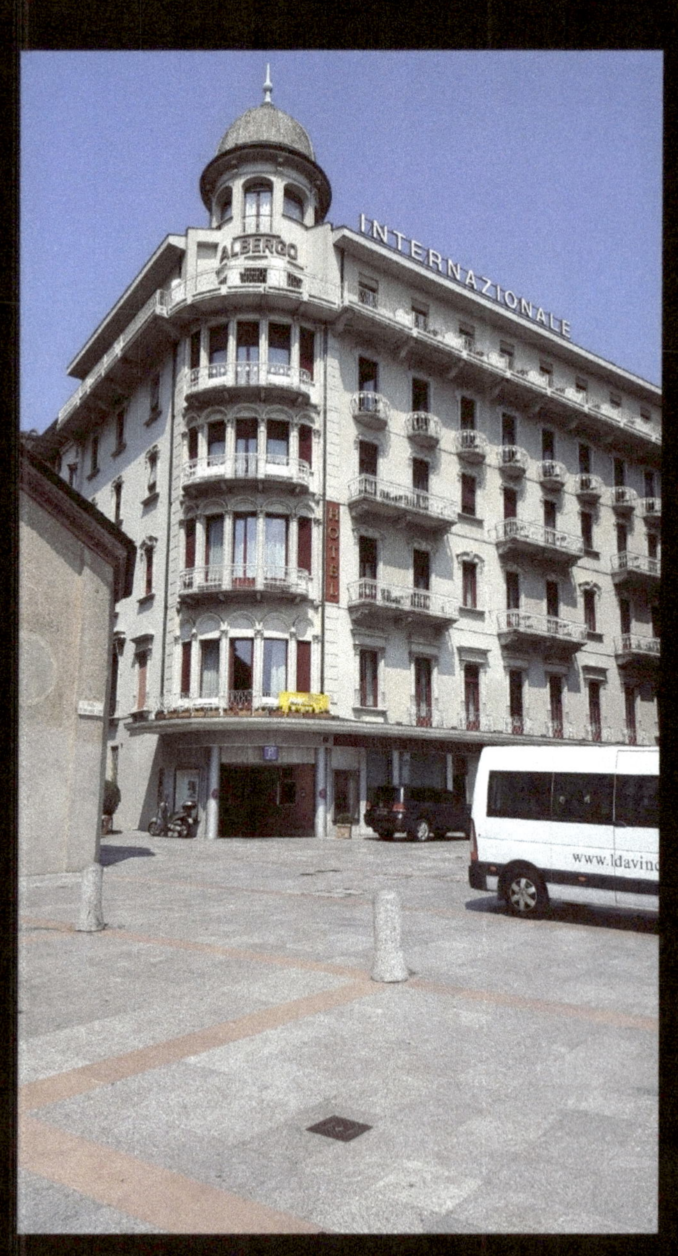

FORMAL GLORY

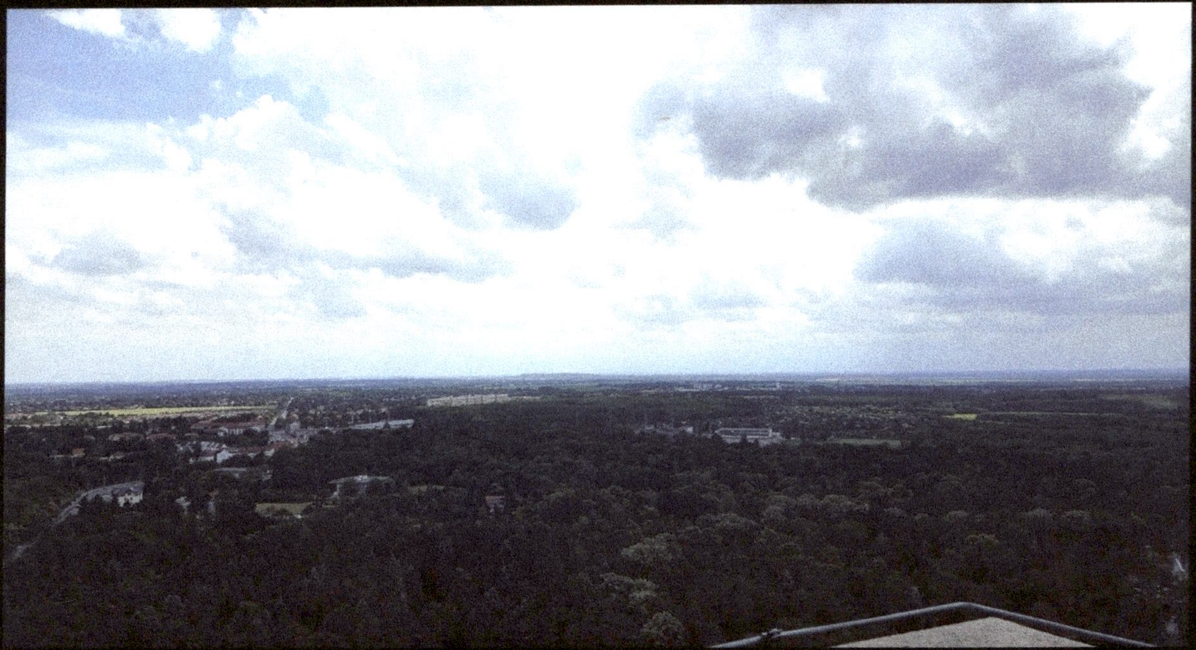

PLATEAU

SERPENTINE

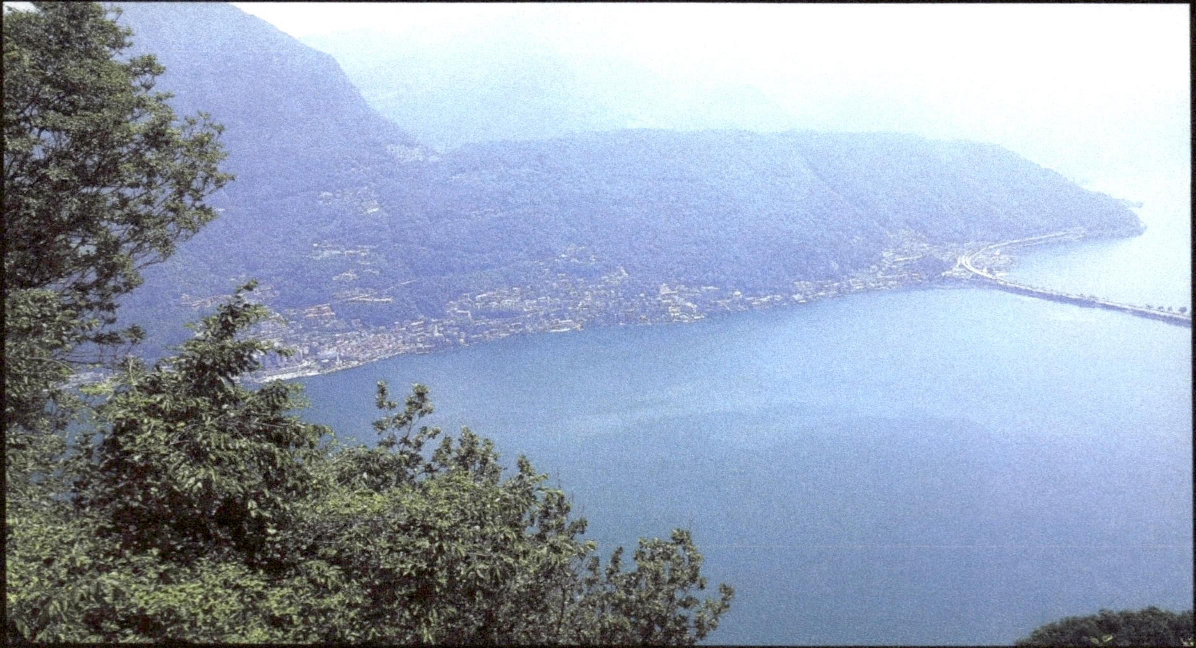

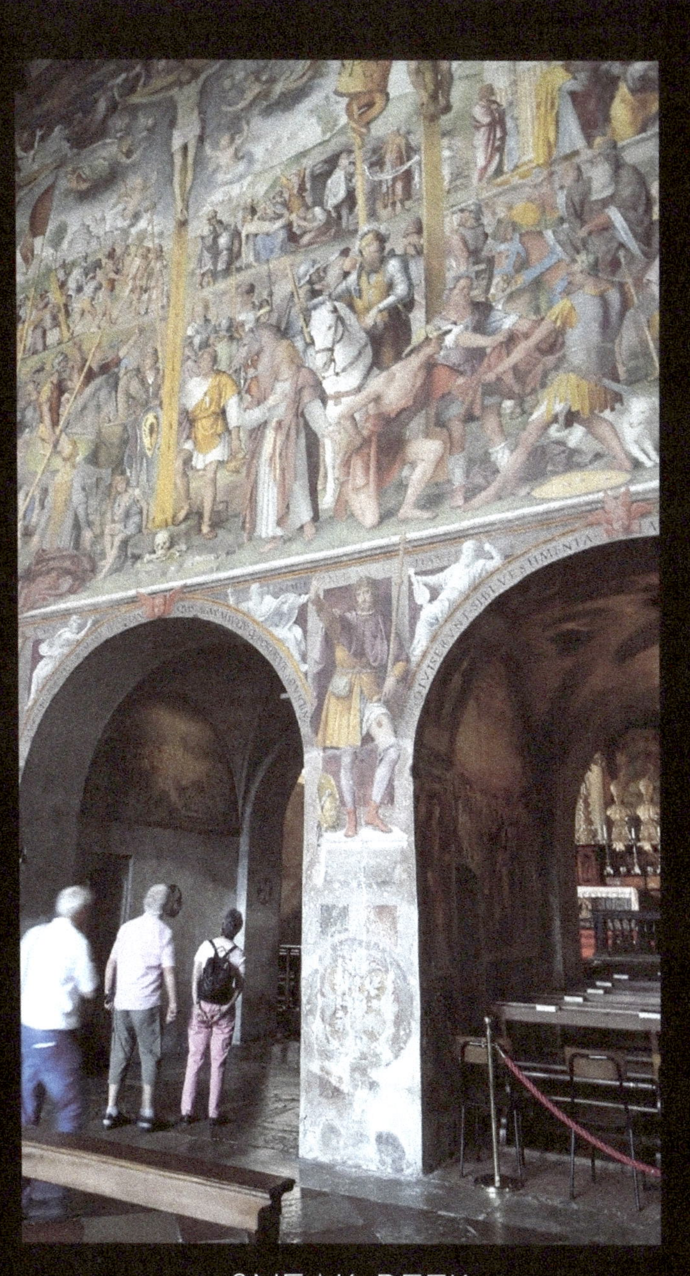

SNEAK PEEK

ROCKET LAUNCH

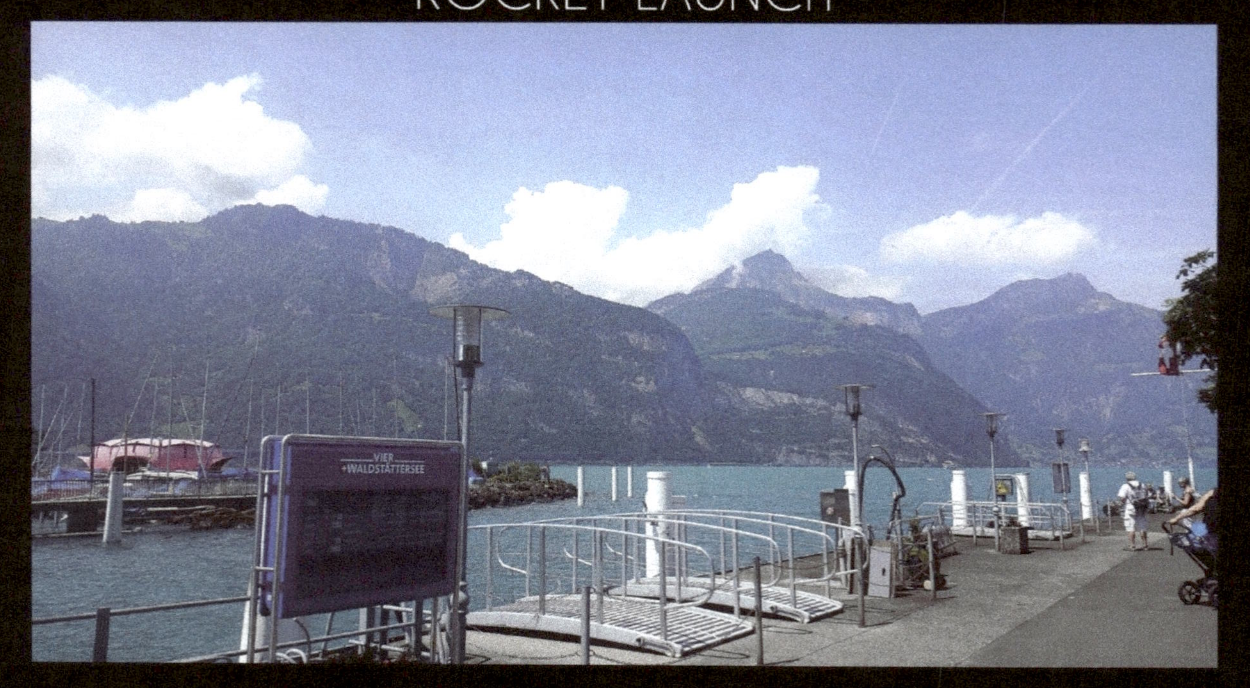

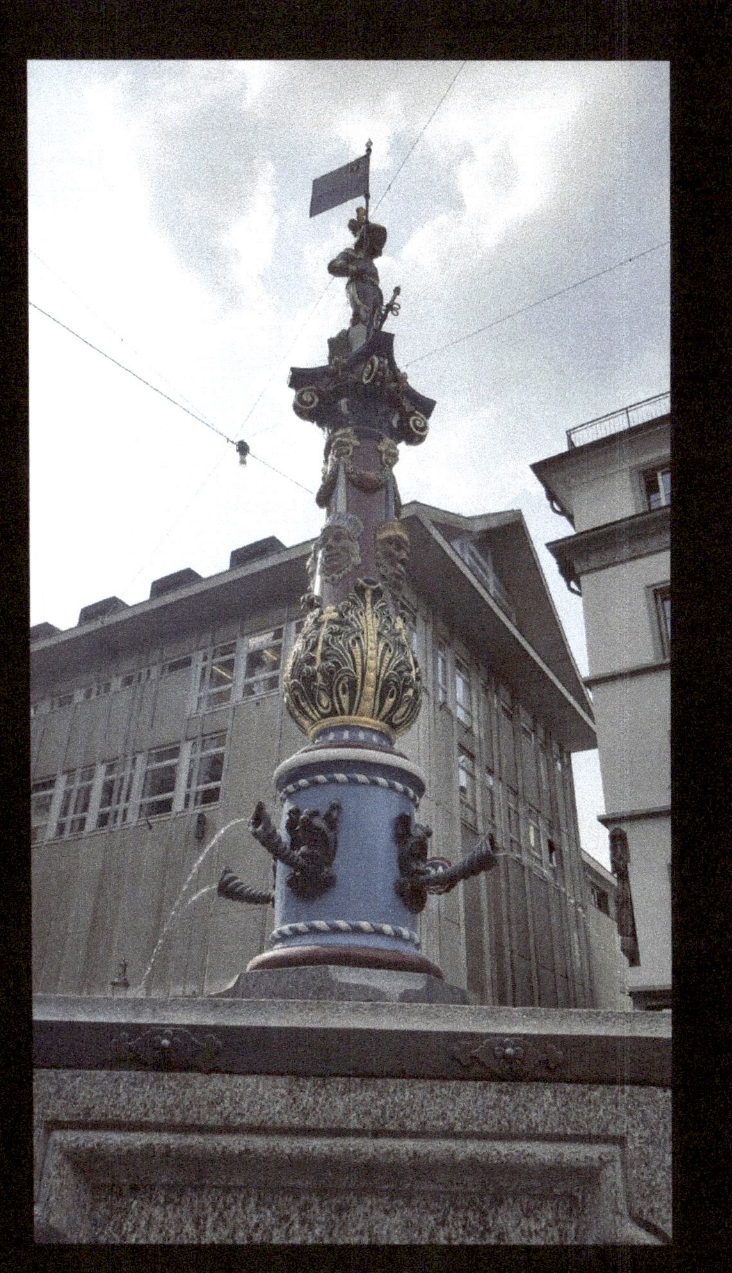

HORNS OF PLENTY

DISAPPEAR

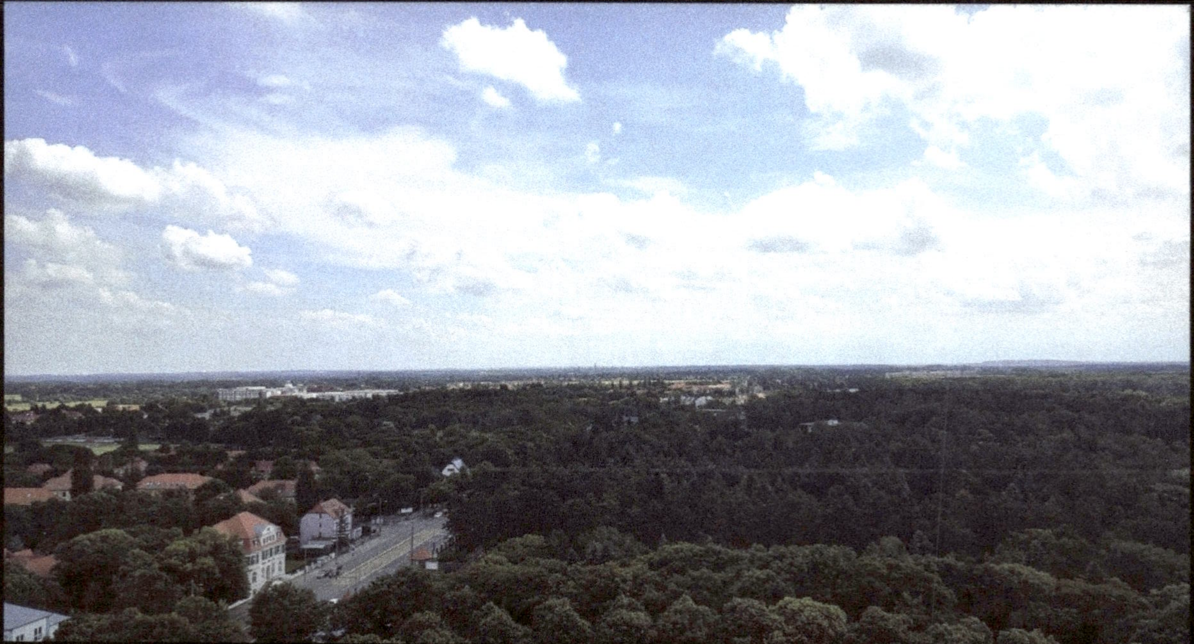

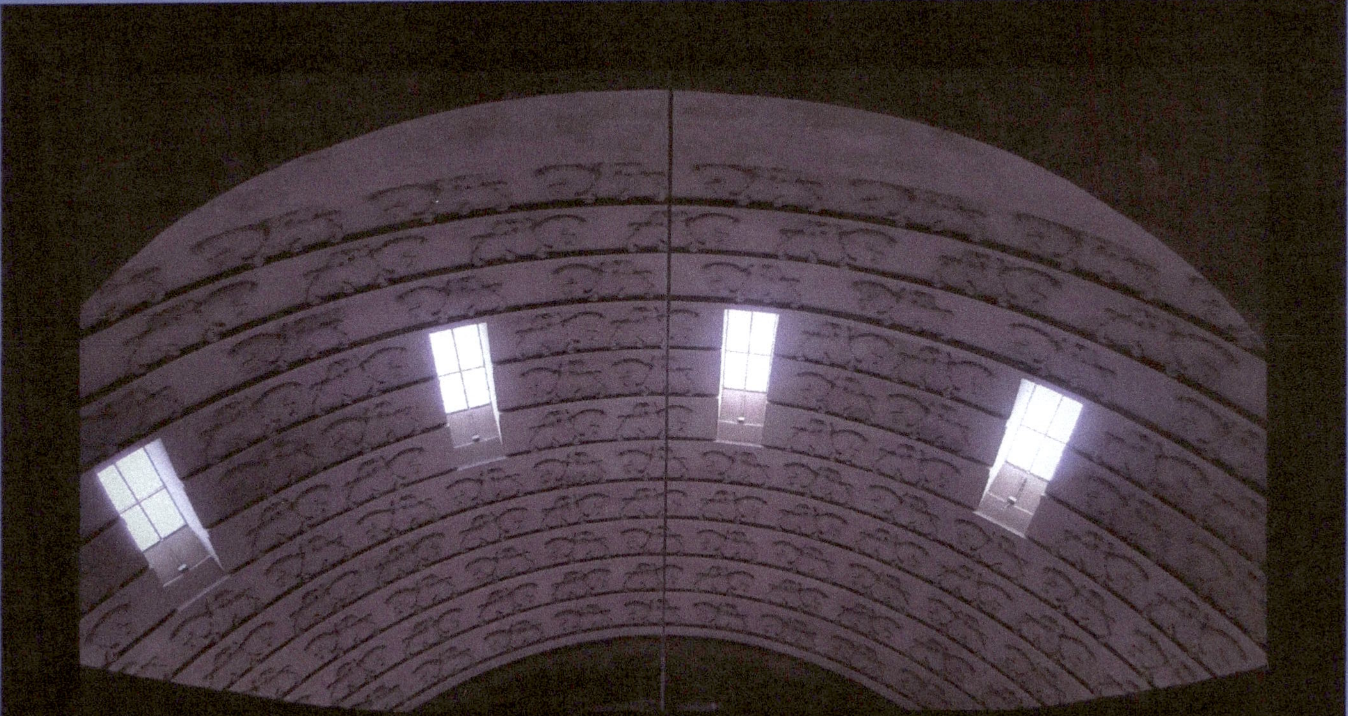

ROGUE ROUGE

PAPAL TIARA

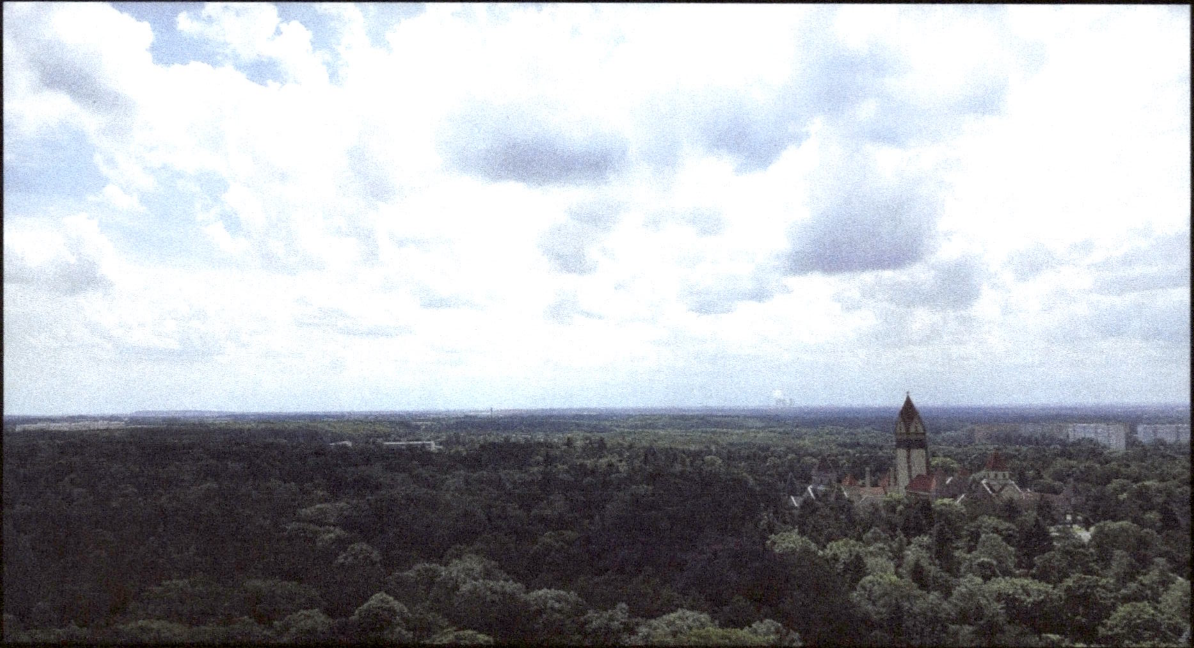

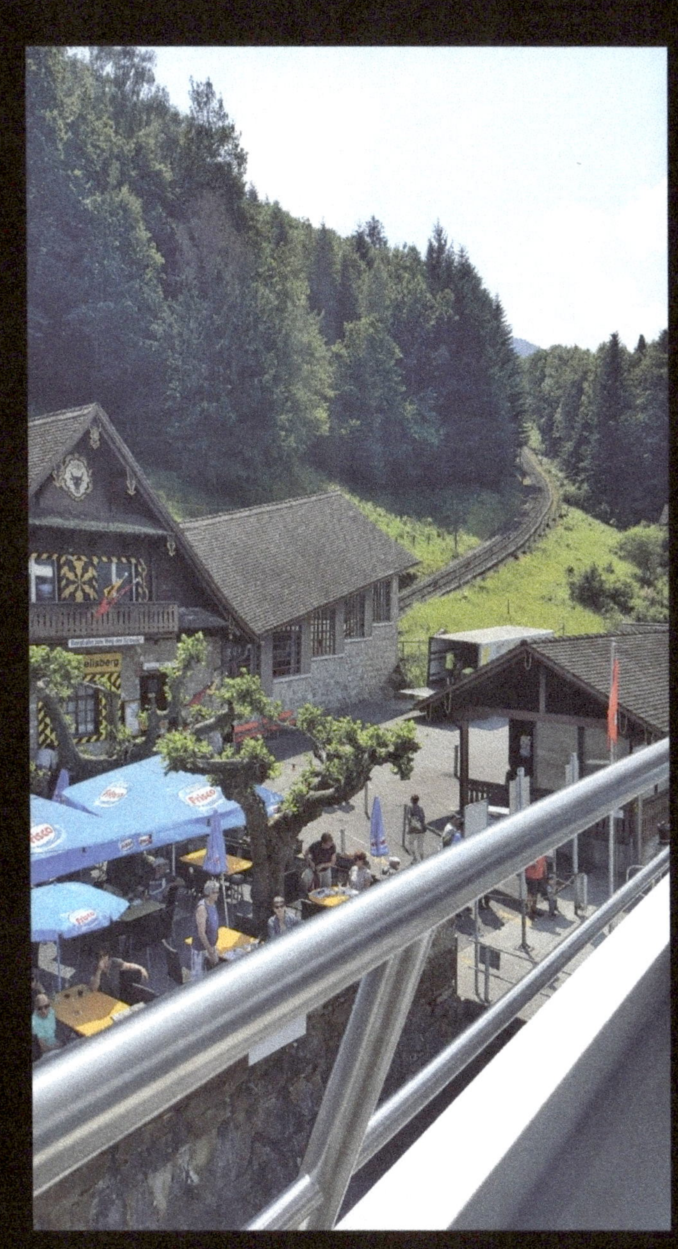

TINY TOWN

CASTLE KEEP

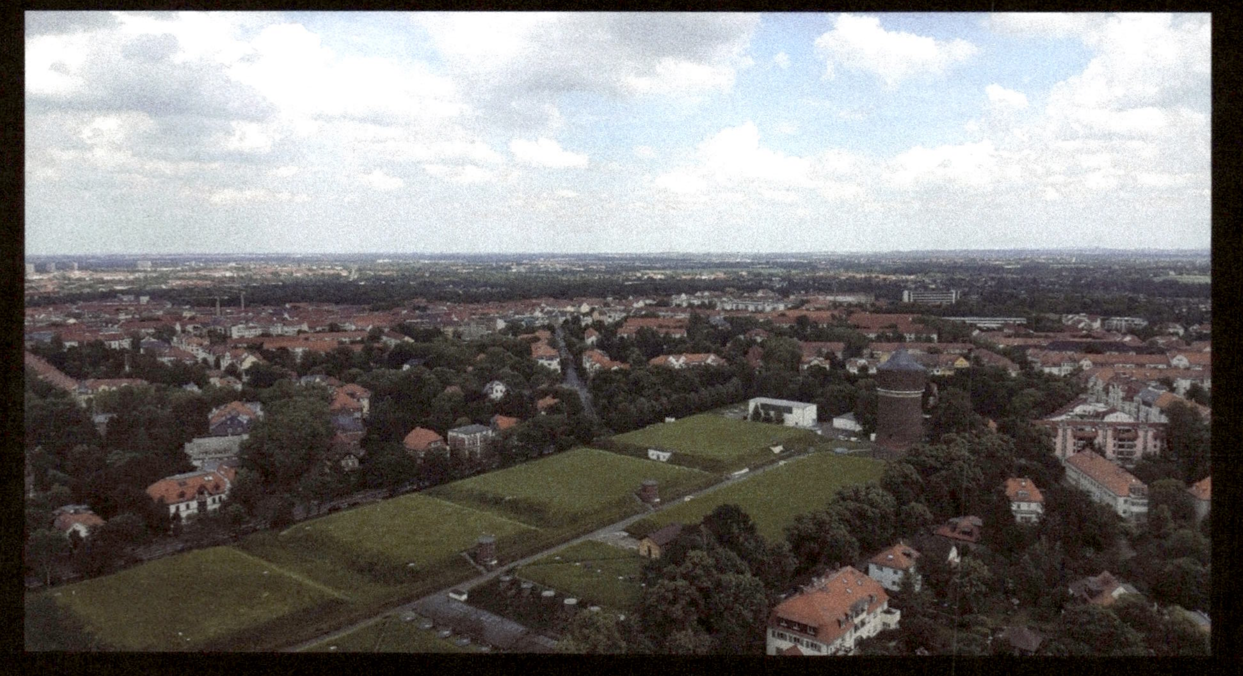

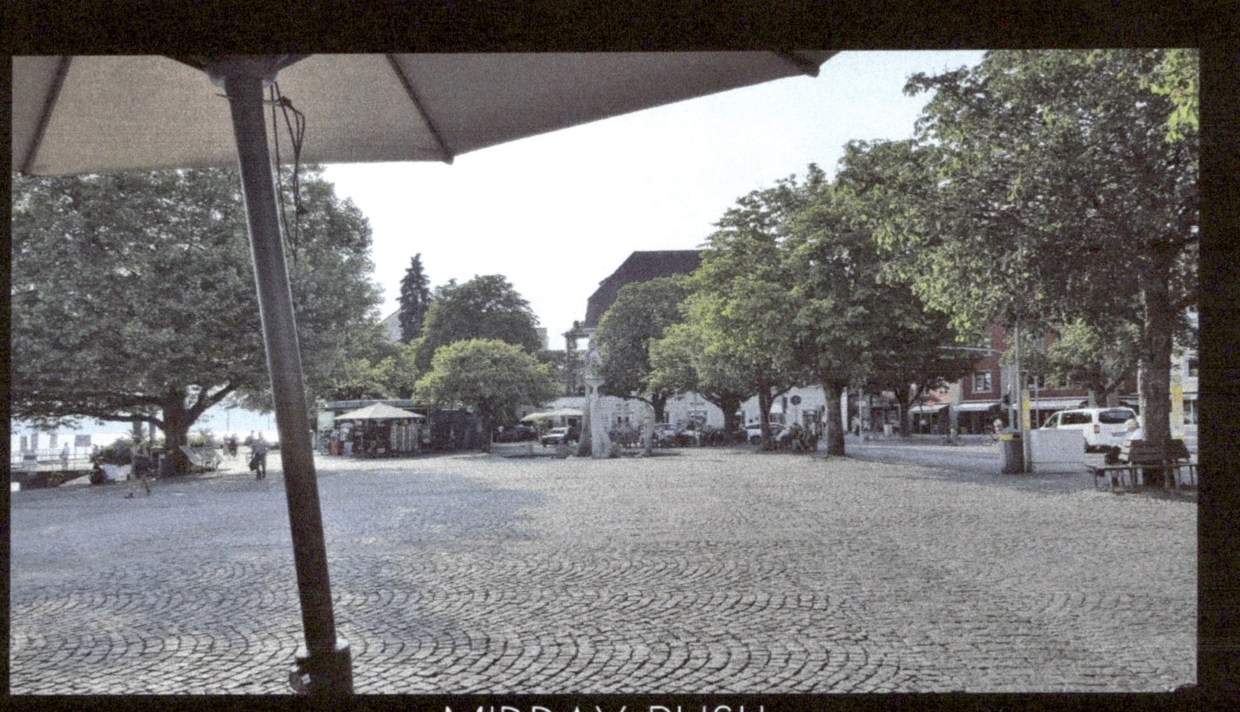

MIDDAY RUSH

HORIZON

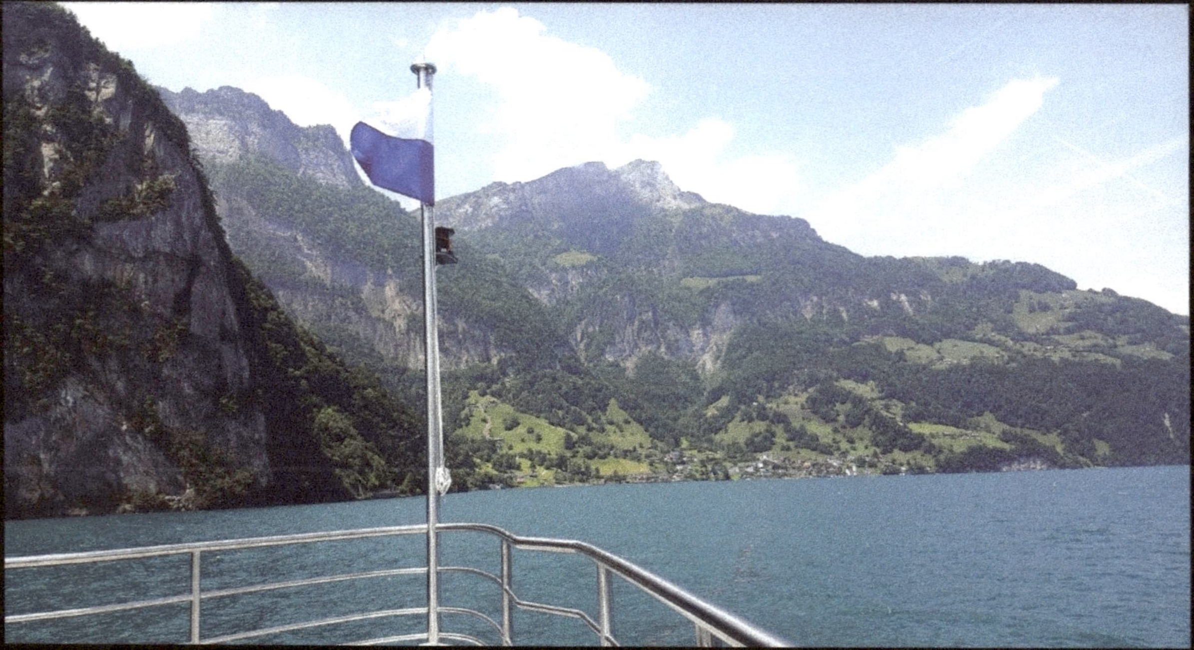

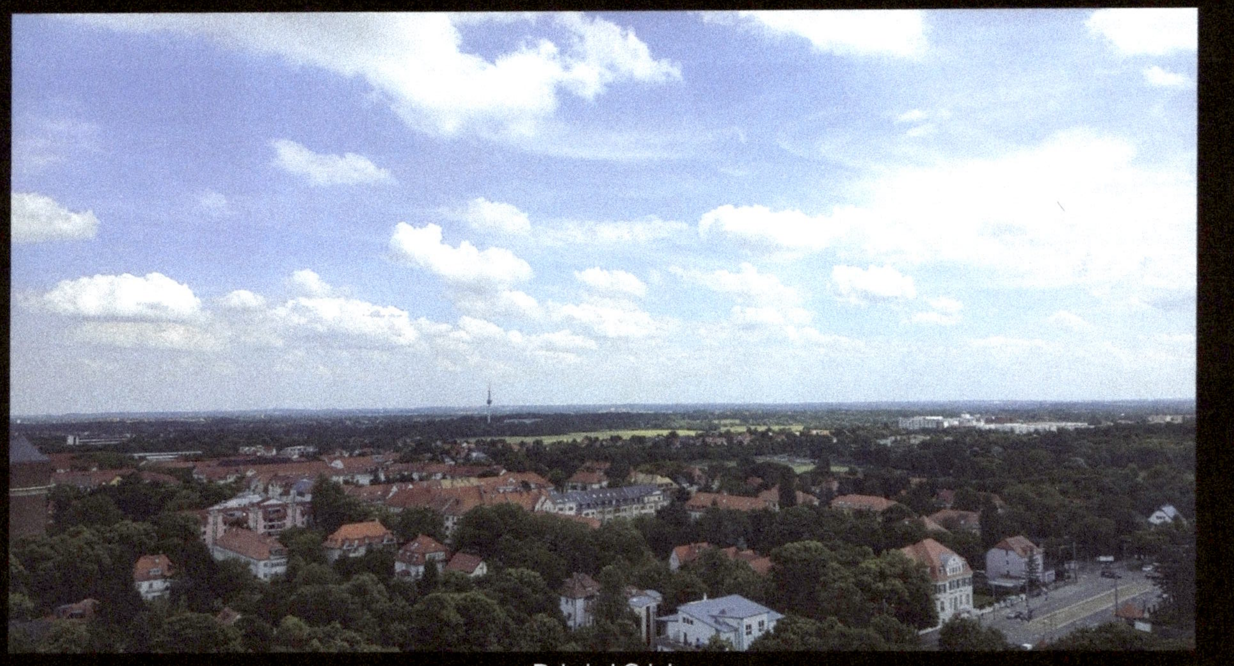

BLUSH

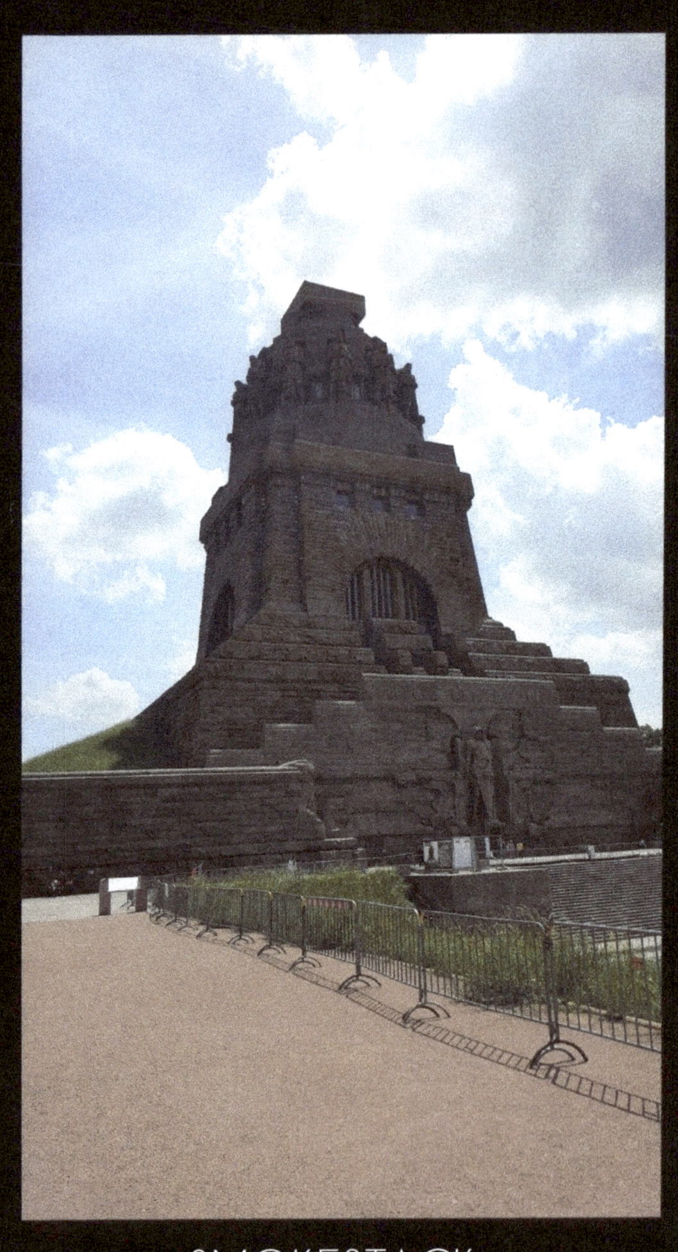

SMOKESTACK

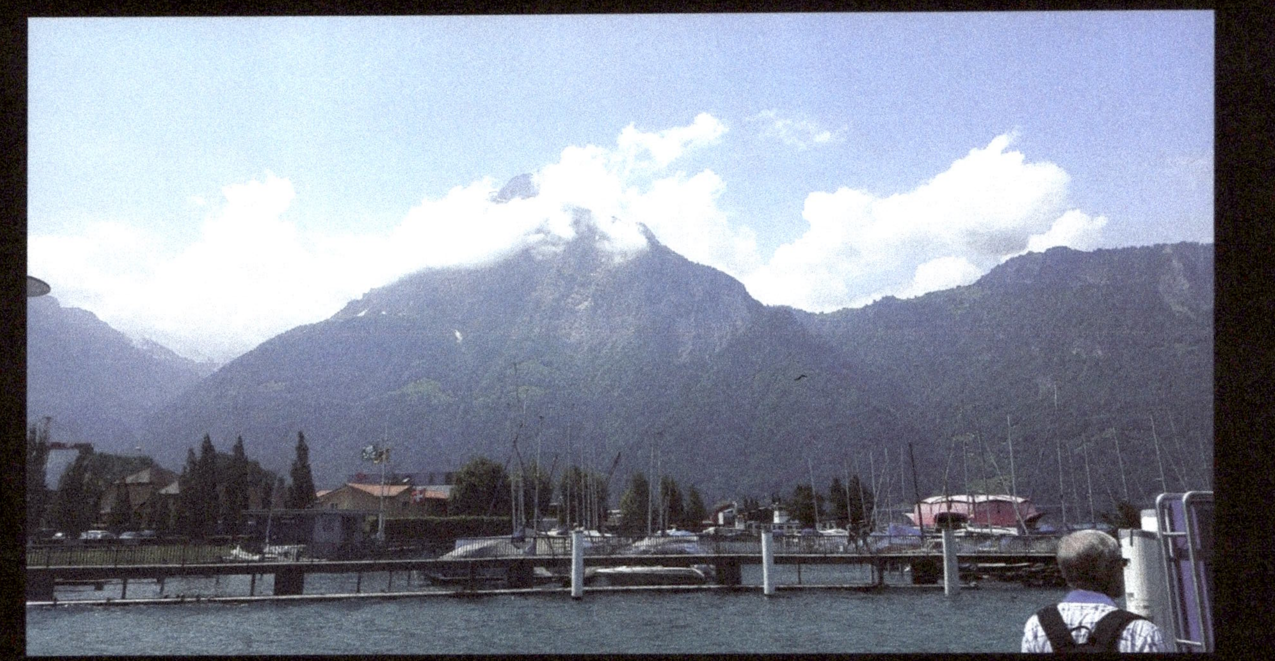

SEVEN VEILS

PEACEFUL

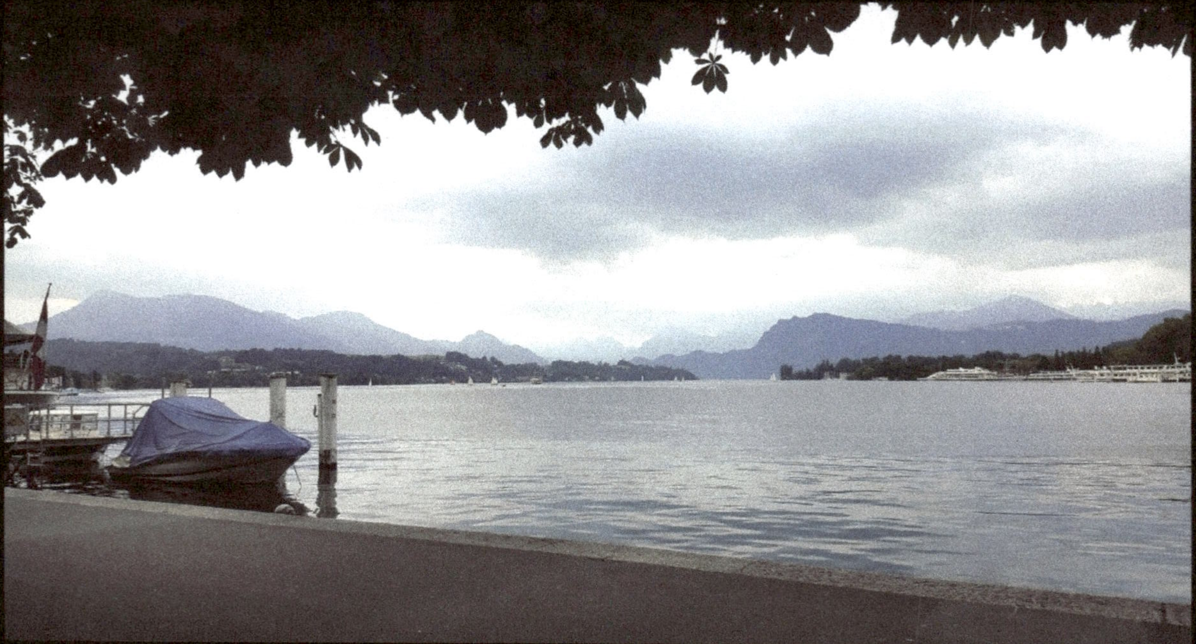

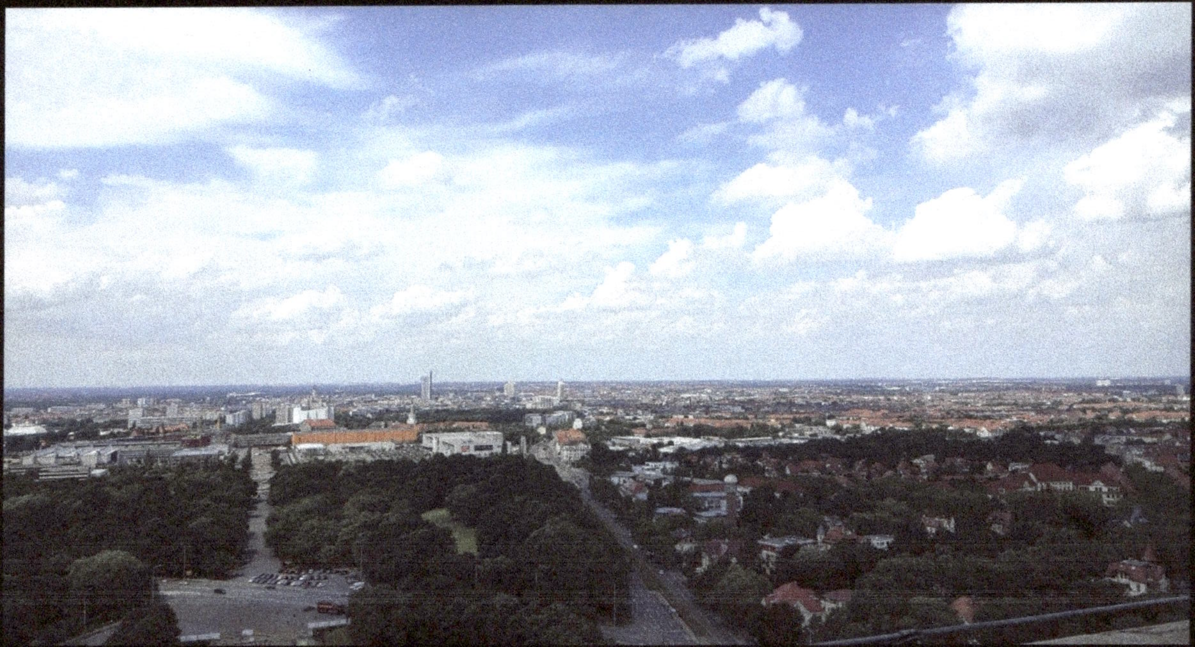

MINGLING

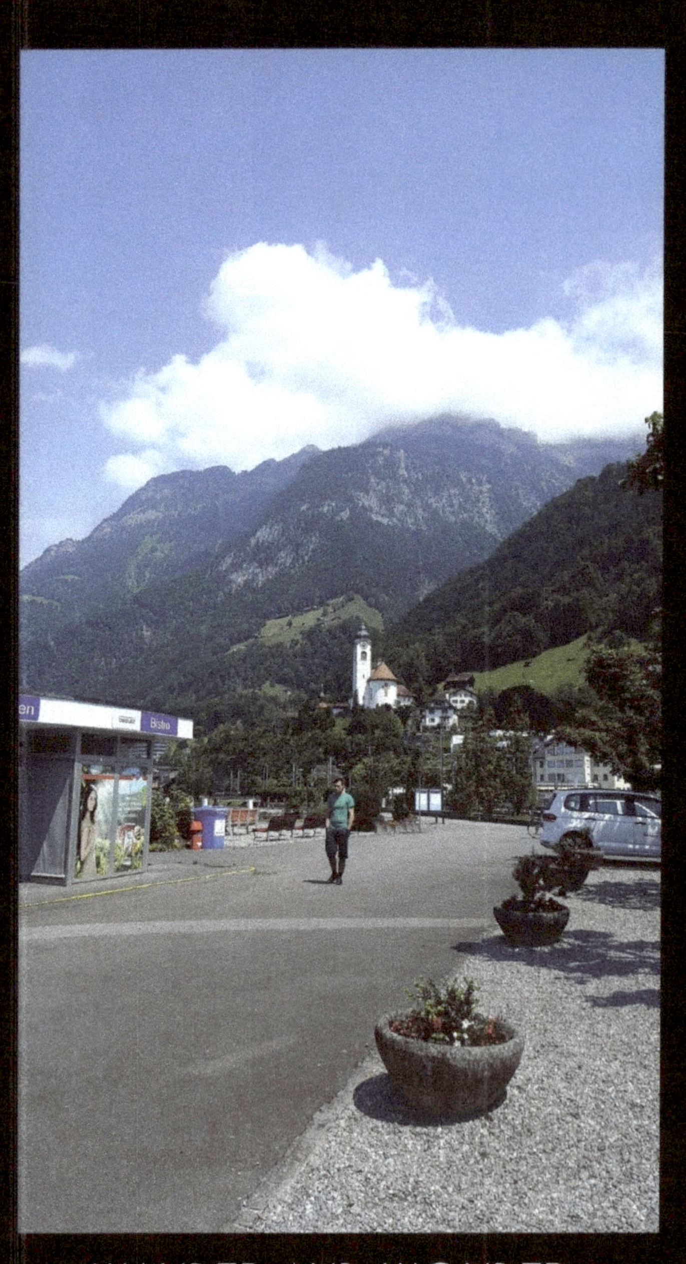
WANDER AND WONDER

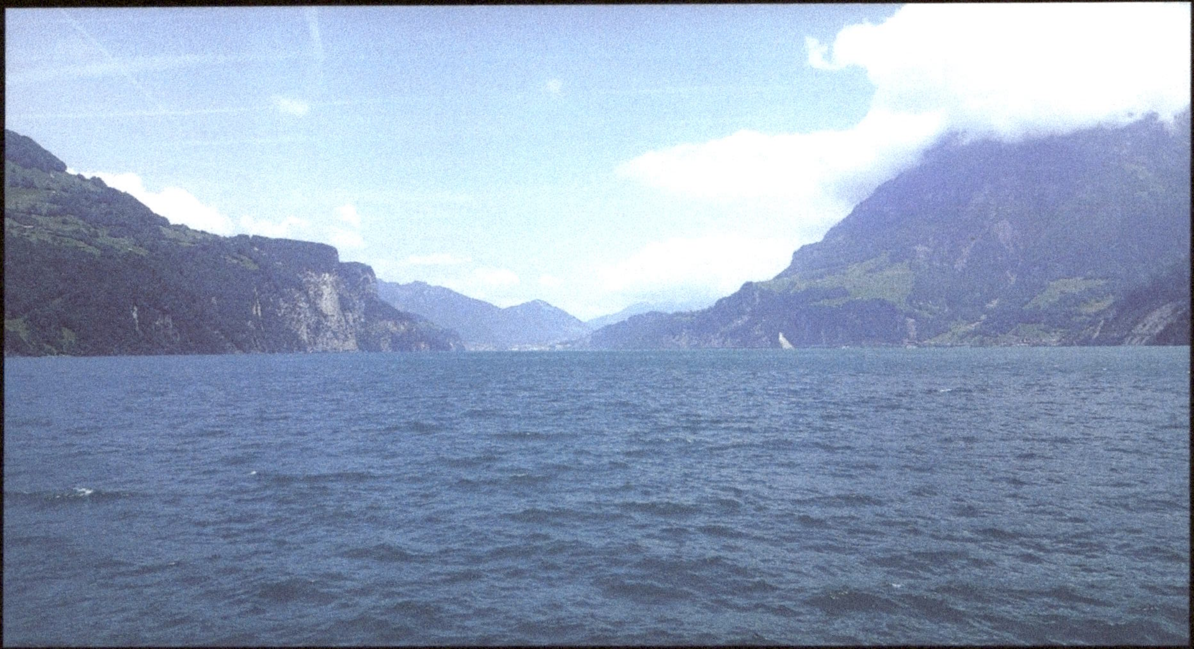

ZIGGURAT

About the Author

Laine Cunningham is an award-winning novelist. Her women's travel adventure memoir *Woman Alone: A Six-Month Journey Through the Australian Outback* appeals to fans of *Wild* and *Eat Pray Love*.

Fiction

The Family Made of Dust

Beloved

Reparation

Nonfiction

Woman Alone

On the Wallaby Track: Australian Words and Phrases

Seven Sisters: Messages from Aboriginal Australia

Writing While Female or Black or Gay

The Zen of Travel
The Zen of Gardening
Zen in the Stable
The Zen of Chocolate
The Zen of Dogs

The Wisdom of Puppies
The Wisdom of Babies
The Wisdom of Weddings

Bikes of Berlin
Necropolises of New Orleans I & II
Ruins of Rome I & II
Ancients of Assisi I & II
Panoramas of Portugal
Nuances of New York
Glimpses of Germany
Impressions of Italy
Altitudes of the Alps
Utopia of the Unicorn
Knights Through the Ages

www.ingramcontent.com/pod-product-compliance
Lightning Source LLC
Chambersburg PA
CBHW050021040726
47599CB00014B/1496